BIOLOGY BASICS Need to Know

Animal Classification

by Ruth Owen
Consultant: Jordan Stoleru
Science Educator

Minneapolis, Minnesota

Credits

Cover and title page, © narvikk/iStock; 5, © Andres Avecedo/Shutterstock; 7, © notsuperstar/Shutterstock, © ILYA AKINSHIN/Shutterstock, © Anan Kaewkhammul/Shutterstock, © Svetlana Foote/Shutterstock, © phatthanasan suporn/Shutterstock, © Krakenimages.com/Shutterstock, © Puttachat Kumkrong/Shutterstock, © Patryk Kosmider/Shutterstock, © Eric Isselee/Shutterstock, © Nejron Photo/Shutterstock, and © Hintau Aliaksei/Shutterstock; 9TL, © Andrej Jakubik/Shutterstock; 9TR, © Sumruay Rattanataipob/Shutterstock; 9BL, © Sergio Photone/Shutterstock; 9BR, © NNER/Shutterstock; 11T, © Prostock-studio/Shutterstock; 11B, © loveyousomuch/Shutterstock; 13, © marshalgonz/Shutterstock; 14, © Julian Popov/Shutterstock; 15, © InkaOne/Shutterstock; 17, © Russell Marshall/Shutterstock; 18, © Brandon Alms/Shutterstock; 21, © Martin Pelanek/Shutterstock; 23T, © Visual Intermezzo/Shutterstock; 23B, © Tran The Ngoc/Shutterstock; 25T, © Rudmer Zwerver/Shutterstock; 25B, © IngeBlessas/Shutterstock; 26–27, © Artush/Shutterstock; 27, © Agami Photo Agency/Shutterstock; and 28, © woolball/Shutterstock.

Bearport Publishing Company Product Development Team

President: Jen Jenson; Director of Product Development: Spencer Brinker; Managing Editor: Allison Juda; Associate Editor: Naomi Reich; Associate Editor: Tiana Tran; Senior Designer: Colin O'Dea; Associate Designer: Elena Klinkner; Associate Designer: Kayla Eggert; Product Development Specialist: Anita Stasson

Library of Congress Cataloging-in-Publication Data is available at www.loc.gov or upon request from the publisher.

ISBN: 979-8-88822-034-4 (hardcover)
ISBN: 979-8-88822-226-3 (paperback)
ISBN: 979-8-88822-349-9 (ebook)

Copyright © 2024 Bearport Publishing Company. All rights reserved. No part of this publication may be reproduced in whole or in part, stored in any retrieval system, or transmitted in any form or by any means, electronic, mechanical, photocopying, recording, or otherwise, without written permission from the publisher.

For more information, write to Bearport Publishing, 5357 Penn Avenue South, Minneapolis, MN 55419.

Contents

The Animal Planet 4

Great Groups 6

No Bones about It 10

Meet the Vertebrates 12

Is It Cold in Here? 16

Backbones below the Water 20

Big Groups, Little Animals 22

Odd Animal Out 24

Something New 26

Animal Characteristics 28

SilverTips for Success 29

Glossary 30

Read More 31

Learn More Online 31

Index 32

About the Author 32

The Animal Planet

Earth is home to tiny fleas and giant blue whales. There are buzzing bees, stunning starfish, terrifying tigers, and much more. In fact, there are almost 9 million different types of animals on Earth. How do we keep track of them all? We can use **classification**.

What is an animal? All animals share a few things in common. They are living things. Animals can move, eat, and have young. All animals need **oxygen** to live.

Great Groups

Scientists sort all living things into groups, or classifications. One of the largest ways to break things down is by kingdom. All animals belong to a single kingdom.

From there, the animal kingdom is divided into smaller groups. Those groups are divided into smaller groups, too. Each time, there are fewer animals.

Other kingdoms group together other living things. There is a kingdom for all plants. Another kingdom has fungi, such as mushrooms. There are even kingdoms for tiny one-celled living things.

Kingdom

Species

Groups get smaller as they are divided. The smallest group is called a species.

Scientists decide what should be grouped together based on **characteristics**. These are how animals look and act. Does a creature have hair, feathers, or scales? How does it have babies? Can we find it flying with wings or swimming with fins? Animals with similar characteristics go together.

The kinds of food an animal eats is also a characteristic. Some animals eat only meat. Others chow down on plants. Many animals eat both meat and plants.

No Bones about It

The animal kingdom is split into **vertebrates** and **invertebrates**. Their difference comes down to bones. Vertebrates have spines, or backbones. Humans are a type of vertebrate.

Invertebrates have no spine or any other bones. This group includes worms, insects, and jellyfish.

Bones give vertebrates their shapes and protect their organs. Bones also connect to muscles to help these animals move. Invertebrates have other ways to do these things.

Meet the Vertebrates

There are five groups, or classes, of vertebrate animals. They are **mammals**, birds, **reptiles**, **amphibians**, and fish. Animals from each class share common characteristics.

Mammals are warm-blooded. They make their own body heat. Mammals also have hair and breathe with lungs. They give birth to babies that drink milk from their mothers' bodies.

Dolphins are mammals.

Some unusual mammals live in water. They must come to the surface to breathe air. Some of these animals have very little hair. Others lose their hair as they grow older.

Birds are another class of warm-blooded vertebrates. Like mammals, they also breathe with lungs.

What makes them different from mammals? Birds lay eggs to have babies. They sit on the eggs until they hatch. Birds also have feathers and wings. Most birds use their wings to fly.

Many bird parents spit up food straight into the beaks of their babies. However, there are a few that make a kind of milk. Pigeons, flamingos, and male emperor penguins feed their chicks this milk-like food.

Is It Cold in Here?

Cold-blooded vertebrates have backbones but cannot make their own warmth. They must get heat from the air or water around them.

Reptiles fall into this group. All reptiles also breathe with lungs. They have either four legs or no legs at all. Scaly skin covers their bodies.

Most reptiles lay eggs. Unlike bird eggs, reptile eggs have tough, rubbery shells. Another big difference is how reptile parents act. They tend to leave the eggs rather than staying with them until the babies hatch.

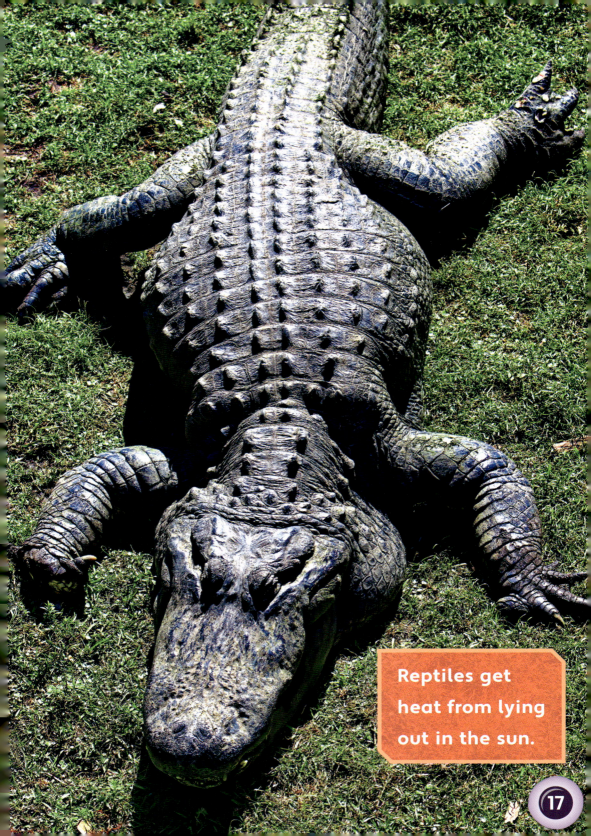

Reptiles get heat from lying out in the sun.

Frogs and toads belong to a class called amphibians. These are cold-blooded vertebrates with moist skin. Amphibians lay soft, jellylike eggs in ponds and streams. The young hatch and start their lives underwater. As they grow, amphibians change dramatically. Most adult amphibians live on land.

Young amphibians can breathe underwater. They often have fins. As they become adults, most grow lungs and legs. They move to dry land where they live out the rest of their lives.

Backbones below the Water

The final class of cold-blooded vertebrates is fish. The most obvious shared characteristic is their home. Fish live in the water. **Gills** allow them to breathe underwater. Most fish have scaly skin and fins for swimming. Some fish give birth to babies, but most lay eggs.

Fish have gills on either side of their heads. These thin slits get oxygen out of the water. Fish cannot breathe on land. Most do not have lungs.

Big Groups, Little Animals

More than 95 percent of the animals on Earth are invertebrates. The majority of those are insects. All insects have an armor-like shell called an **exoskeleton**. Their bodies are broken up into three parts, and they have six legs.

Spiders are also invertebrates with exoskeletons. However, they have two-part bodies and eight legs.

As a spider grows, its exoskeleton does not. What happens when things get too tight? The spider breaks out of its old exoskeleton. Underneath, there is a newer, bigger one.

Odd Animal Out

Characteristics help with most classifications. However, some oddball animals are harder to place. Bats are warm-blooded, furry, and have babies that they feed milk. However, they are the only mammals that can fly.

A platypus is a mammal, too. But this strange creature has a bill, lives partly in water, and lays eggs.

The platypus and the bat share most things in common with mammals. However, they split from others quickly as mammals are broken into more specific groups.

Something New

What's the point of putting animals into classifications? It makes it easier to know about each animal. How will it look and behave? Check out other animals in its classification group! This helps to know what to expect thanks to classification.

In 2021, scientists told the world about a new type of reptile. It's a chameleon that is smaller than a coin. Like all reptiles, it is cold-blooded and has scales.

Animal Characteristics

These are some of the characteristics of the main classes of animals.

MAMMALS
- Hair or fur
- Vertebrates
- Warm-blooded
- Feed young milk

BIRDS
- Feathers and wings
- Vertebrates
- Warm-blooded

REPTILES
- Scaly skin
- Vertebrates
- Cold-blooded

FISH
- Scaly skin, fins, and a tail
- Vertebrates
- Cold-blooded
- Live in water

INSECTS
- Invertebrates with exoskeletons
- Six legs and three body parts
- Cold-blooded

AMPHIBIANS
- Moist skin
- Vertebrates
- Cold-blooded
- Live in water when young and on land when adults

SPIDERS
- Invertebrates with exoskeletons
- Eight legs and two body parts
- Cold-blooded

SilverTips for SUCCESS

★ SilverTips for REVIEW

Review what you've learned. Use the text to help you.

Define key terms

- characteristics
- class
- classification
- invertebrate
- vertebrate

Check for understanding

Describe what animal characteristics are and how we use them.

What is the difference between a vertebrate and an invertebrate?

How do cold-blooded and warm-blooded animals differ?

Think deeper

Think of the characteristics of an animal. What group do you think it belongs to? Name another animal in that group.

★ SilverTips on TEST-TAKING

- **Make a study plan.** Ask your teacher what the test is going to cover. Then, set aside time to study a little bit every day.

- **Read all the questions carefully.** Be sure you know what is being asked.

- **Skip any questions** you don't know how to answer right away. Mark them and come back later if you have time.

Glossary

amphibians cold-blooded animals with backbones that live part of their lives in water and part on land

characteristics typical qualities or features

classification the act of putting things into groups based upon their characteristics

exoskeleton the hard outer covering on the body of an insect or spider

gills body parts of some animals that let them get oxygen underwater

invertebrates animals that don't have backbones or any other bones

mammals warm-blooded animals with backbones that have hair, give birth to live young, and feed their babies milk

oxygen a gas that all animals need to breathe

reptiles cold-blooded animals with backbones and scales

vertebrates animals with backbones

Read More

Huddleston, Emma. *Animal Classification (Discover Biology).* Minneapolis: ABDO Publishing, 2022.

Hughes, Sloane. *20 Things You Should Know about Mammal Adaptations (Did You Know? Animal Adaptations).* New York: PowerKids Press, 2023.

Seigel, Rachel. *Amphibians (Field Guides).* Minneapolis: ABDO Publishing, 2023.

Learn More Online

1. Go to **www.factsurfer.com** or scan the QR code below.
2. Enter "**Animal Classification**" into the search box.
3. Click on the cover of this book to see a list of websites.

Index

amphibians 12, 18, 28

babies 8, 12, 14, 16, 20, 24

birds 12, 14, 16, 28

characteristics 8, 12, 20, 24, 28

cold-blooded 16, 18, 20, 27–28

exoskeleton 22, 28

fish 12, 20, 28

food 8, 14

gills 20–21

insects 10, 22, 28

invertebrates 10–11, 22, 28

kingdoms 6–7, 10

mammals 12–14, 24, 28

oxygen 4, 20

reptiles 12, 16–17, 27–28

spiders 22, 28

vertebrates 10–12, 14, 16, 18, 20, 28

warm-blooded 12, 14, 24, 28

About the Author

Ruth Owen has been working on books for more than 12 years. She lives in Cornwall, England, just minutes from the ocean. Ruth loves writing books about animals and nature.